Kaliningrad

Lithuania

Russian Feder

Suwalki

Olsztyn

Suchowola

Łomża

Białystok

Belarus

Official nam	
Official lang	
Area:	
Coastline:	
Climate:	Temperate
Population:	38,500,000
Capital:	Warsaw
Religions:	Roman Catholic
Currency:	1 Polish złoty = US $.36 = CAN $.36

Bialowieza

Bug

Vistula

WARSAW

Brest

Biala
Podlaska

Vistula

Radom

Pulawy

Lublin

Uza

0 - 200 m = 0 - 656 ft

200 - 500 m = 656 - 1640 ft

500 - 1000 m = 1640 - 3281 ft

1000 - 1500 m = 3281 - 4921 ft

1500 - 2000 m = 4921 - 6562 ft

Ostrowiec
Swietokrzyski

Zamość

Ukraine

Kraków

Tarnów

Rzeszów

Lvov

Wieliczka

Nowy
Sacz

0   50 km

0   50 miles

Zako-
pane

Slovakia

Looking at Europe

Poland

Jan Kądziołka
Tadeusz Wojciechowski

The Oliver Press, Inc.
Minneapolis

This edition published in 2011 by The Oliver Press, Inc.
Charlotte Square
5707 West 36th Street
Minneapolis, MN 55416-2510

Published by arrangement with KIT Publishers, The Netherlands, and
The Evans Publishing Group, London, UK, 2006

Library of Congress Cataloging-in-Publication Data
Kadziolka, Jan.
  [Op bezoek in Polen. English]
  Poland / Jan Kadziolka, Tadeusz Wojciechowski.
      p. cm. -- (Looking at Europe)
  Includes bibliographical references and index.
  ISBN 978-1-881508-89-2 (alk. paper)
  1. Poland--Juvenile literature. I. Wojciechowski, Tadeusz. II. Title.
  DK4147.K33 2010
  943.8--dc22
                                                          2009035350

Text: Jan Kądziołka and Tadeusz Wojciechowski
Photographs: Jan Willem Bultje
Translation: Jeske Nelissen
U.S. editing: Anna Aman
Design and Layout: Grafisch Ontwerpbureau Agaatsz BNO, Meppel, The Netherlands
Cover: Icon Productions, Minneapolis, USA
Cartography: Armand Haye, Amsterdam, The Netherlands
Production: J & P Far East Productions, Soest, The Netherlands

Picture Credits
Photographs: Jan Willem Bultje
p. 8 (b), 16 (b), 21 (t), 25 (b), 28 (t), 29, 35 (b), 40 (b), 41 (t), 42, 43 (t), 44, 45, 46, and 47
Polish Tourist Organization; p. 19 (t) and 25 (t) Janek Skarzynski; p. 14 (t) Stanislaxw Ciok;
p. 38 (t) and 39 (t) Piotr Krzyzannowsky Przemyslaw Pokrycki: Epa Photo; p. 22 (b) ©
Raymond Gehman/CORBIS; p. 27 (b) © Paul Almasy/CORBIS; p. 30 (t) © Raymond
Gehman/CORBIS; p. 37(t) © Raymond Gehman/CORBIS; p. 41(b) © Steve Raymer/CORBIS

ISBN 978-1-881508-89-2
Printed in The United States of America
14 13 12 11 11   5 4 3 2 1

Contents

Introduction

Poland is a fascinating country filled with diverse landscapes such as mountains, plains, rivers, and forests. The country is also filled with beautiful architecture and rich traditions. Poland has a long and varied history, including periods of great prosperity and severe hardship.

To Poland's north lies the Baltic Sea, but the rest of the country, one of the largest in Europe, is surrounded by land. Germany and the Czech Republic are to the west, Slovakia and Ukraine to the south, Belarus and Lithuania to the east, and Kaliningrad, a region of the Russian Federation (Russia), is to the northeast. The capital and largest city is Warsaw. Most of Poland is made up of lowlands, except the far south of the country, which is lined by the Carpathian and Sudeten Mountains. Across the lowland regions are many ancient lakes and forests. Throughout Poland, a number of national parks and nature reserves have been established to protect the plant and animal life of the countryside.

Poland's almost landlocked position in the middle of Europe has caused problems during much of its history. At various points in the past, Poland has fallen under the control of its neighboring countries. This happened most recently at the beginning of World War II, when Germany invaded Poland and

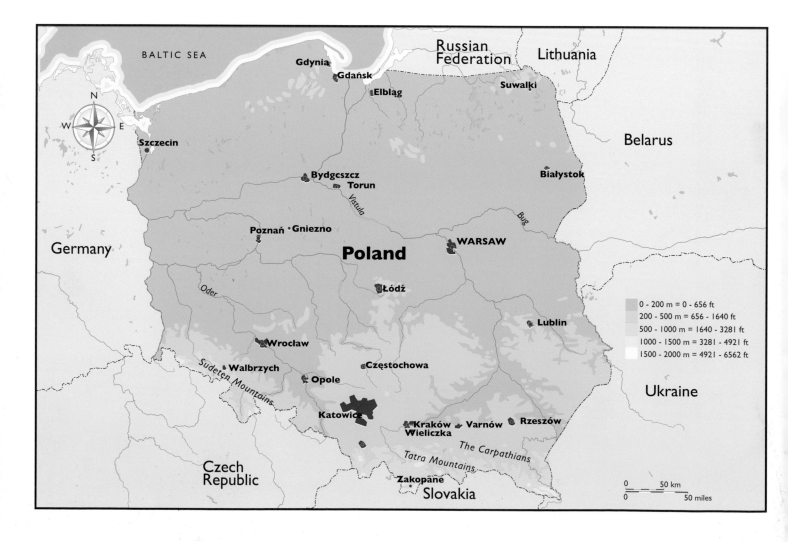

occupied the country for six years. Each time, however, the people have fought to regain their independence. Perhaps because of this, the Poles have a strong sense of national identity and are proud of their history, culture, traditions, and beliefs.

In recent years, Poland's fortunes have begun to rise. It is still not a wealthy country like those in Western Europe, but the government has introduced many reforms, including modernizing industry, improving transportation, and encouraging more trade with other countries. Poland has accomplished this last reform through joining world organizations such as NATO and the European Union (EU).

▲ The majority of Polish people are Roman Catholics, and one of the most famous Poles was Pope John Paul II.

▼ The high street in Gdańsk, showing some of Poland's colorful architecture and thriving city life

History

The territory that is now Poland was once home to various tribes that ventured there from neighboring lands. By the ninth century, some tribes had begun to rule the Slavs of the region, and the roots of the Polish nation were sown. The Polish state itself was established near the end of the tenth century by Mieszko I, a duke from the Piast family.

In the Middle Ages, Poland was a huge and powerful state spanning almost 390,000 square miles. The sixteenth century saw the height of Poland's greatness, and this period became known as a golden age in the country's history. Art and culture flourished, and the people prospered. Evidence of this can still be seen in some of the magnificent buildings that have survived in Poland. Many of these can be found in Kraków, which once was the country's capital city. Among the most famous buildings are the Wawel Castle, where the Polish kings used to live, and the Mariacki Church (Church of the Virgin Mary).

▼ *The most striking features of the Mariacki Church in Kraków are the two towers. The taller tower (left) has a spire topped with a gold-plated crown.*

▲ *The market square in Kraków is the largest in Europe. It was designed in 1257, and although the buildings around it are more recent, they still have the original medieval cellars.*

This success, however, was not to last. By the end of the eighteenth century, three of Poland's neighboring countries – Russia, Prussia, and Austria – had agreed to take over Poland and divide the land between them. This was known as the "Partitions of Poland." When the last Partition took place, in 1795, the country completely lost its independence, and the state of Poland ceased to exist.

Over the next few years, the people of Poland struggled for survival and freedom. They threw out a challenge to the rest of Europe, saying:

Poland has not yet succumbed, as long as we remain. What the foe by force has seized, sword in hand we'll gain.

These words, along with the folk tune called the *Mazurek*, became the national anthem.

In the Middle Ages, there were religious wars in several countries across Western Europe. Many people suffered and died for their beliefs, often being burnt at the stake. Throughout this time, Poland was famous for its religious tolerance, and became known as "the state without stakes." In 1791, Poland was the first country in Europe and the second in the world (after the U.S.) to adopt its own democratic constitution. Poland's history also shows that its people understood the benefits of international cooperation. As early as 1569, Poland established the Lublin Union with Lithuania, which joined "the free with the free, the equal with the equal." Under the terms of the union, Poland and Lithuania remained independent states but were joined by their alliance and a ruler. The state was called the "Republic of Two Nations."

▲ *The famous Polish writer Henryk Sienkiewicz won the Nobel Prize for Literature in 1905. He was born in the Russian part of Poland and his family took part in the struggles for independence.*

▼ *Conditions were difficult in Poland during World War II. More than six million Poles were killed and around 2.5 million more were sent to do forced labor in Germany.*

Russia had gained the biggest part of Poland in the Partitions, so the Polish legions fighting for the country's freedom focused on the Russian tsar. In November 1830, an uprising occurred in the city of Warsaw, which was occupied by the Russians. This was called the November Revolution and it lasted for a year. Initially, the Poles managed to drive the Russians out of Warsaw, but by 1831 the city had been retaken and the Poles defeated.

Over the next few decades, uprisings occurred across Austrian and Prussian territories. The biggest and most tragic of these was the January Uprising, which began in 1863. During these rebellions, thousands of Poles perished on battlefields or were executed by shooting or hanging. Even more Poles died in prisons and in the freezing cold and inhumane conditions of Siberia, where they were deported.

After the uprisings were suppressed, emigration started. Thousands of Poles went into exile to escape the harsh conditions of life under occupation. Even though they had been defeated, the Polish people tried to keep their national identity. They did this by continuing to speak their own language and by maintaining their own traditions and beliefs.

World War I

In 1914, World War I broke out. Because the countries responsible for the Partitions stood against each other in this new conflict, the Poles realized that their enemies were weaker than they had been in

◀ Veterans who fought in the Polish army against the German occupation still have annual memorial gatherings.

▼ A statue of Józef Piłsudski in Łodź. Piłsudski was briefly imprisoned, but when Poland gained independence in 1918 he returned to lead his country.

years. They saw an opportunity to strike back and hoped they could win their independence after generations of occupation.

Józef Piłsudski, an activist for the independence movement and future leader of the nation, organized the Polish legions. They initiated the fight against Russia and were also followed by Polish divisions that had formed in France. Other countries began to pay attention when famous Poles, such as the writer and Nobel Prize winner Henryk Sienkiewicz and the pianist Ignacy Paderewski, raised awareness of the plight of the Polish people.

The road to independence

In November 1918, after 123 years of being controlled by other countries, Poland was finally granted its independence. Piłsudski was made head of state and the long process of rebuilding began. Large parts of the country and much of its beautiful architecture had been destroyed.

Poland did not enjoy its hard-won freedom for long. In September 1939, Germany invaded Poland and World War II began. Poland was partitioned once again, this time between Germany and Russia. Despite the collapse of their army, many Poles fled the country and joined the armies opposing Germany. At the end of World War II, leaders of the allied countries held conferences to decide how to control the nations they had fought, and also what to do with the countries previously occupied. The three great powers – the Soviet Union, the United States, and the United Kingdom – established new borders for Poland, which included land that before the war had been Germany's. The victorious allies gave Poland over to the influence of communist Soviet Russia.

When the borders changed, millions of Poles moved from the eastern territories to the west. It was nearly half a century before the Soviet influence in Poland declined. Several factors played a part in this. Two of the most important were the social movement known as Solidarity, and the influence of the Polish Pope John Paul II (see page 47). A new constitution was introduced in 1997. Since then, Poland has improved international relations by taking an active part in many world organizations (see page 5).

The country

Poland's landscape may be roughly divided into three parts: the lowlands, the uplands, and the mountainous regions. Ancient rivers and lakes can be found all over the countryside, and about 50 percent of the land is arable.

The weather in Poland can vary, but in general the climate is pleasant. In the capital, Warsaw, the average temperature in the hottest month (July) is 66°F. In the coldest month (January), it can drop to 26°F. Across much of the country, rainfall is quite low, which means that often there is not enough water to cultivate crops efficiently. This is a particular problem in parts of central Poland. In the mountainous regions in the south of the country, however, there is a lot of water – more than enough for the people living there.

Landscape

Much of the northern and central parts of Poland consist of flat plains, or lowlands. Thousands of years ago, this area was covered by a massive ice sheet, which moved southward and then back again as the climate changed. It left behind hundreds of deposits containing clay, sand and gravel, and "random" boulders scattered across the landscape. Some of these deposits were left in small hills and ridges called moraines. The movement of the ice sheet also created pits in the ground, which grew to become broad river beds.

▲ All across the north of Poland, bordered by the Baltic Sea, there are sandy beaches. Although it rarely gets extremely hot in Poland, the summer climate is perfect for sunbathing.

Rivers

Today, tributaries of the Oder and Vistula rivers still flow westward through these ancient river beds. These are the two largest rivers in Poland and they both flow into the Baltic Sea.

The Vistula flows freely through a series of dams across the middle of the country. Its banks have only been strengthened where it flows through towns. It can be navigated only by smaller boats downstream. The Oder, on the other hand, is controlled through most of its course, which means it can be used for transporting goods between cities and towns.

◄ In the lowland areas left after the retreat of the ice sheet, windblown sand has created these large coastal dunes.

Although the water level in Polish rivers can change, it is usually quite low. Floods normally occur only in springtime, when the snow thaws, and at the beginning of summer, when there is more rainfall than at any other time of year.

In 1997, the levels of rainfall were higher than usual and caused a major flood in the Oder Basin. It was so severe that it became known as "the flood of the century." More than 1,000 towns and villages were flooded; 1,864 miles of roads, 1,243 miles of railway lines and 944 bridges were completely destroyed. The Oder is controlled, which means that in some places it is very narrow and flows through a series of locks. During the flood, these could not contain the sudden surge of water. Around the Vistula River, floodwaters poured over meadows in between the dams. However, because these areas are largely uninhabited, the damage was less severe.

▲ In 1997, the Vistula River flooded, causing extensive damage to many towns and cities. Here the waters flood the streets of Kraków.

The lowlands

There are three different regions that make up the Polish lowlands. The northern part is the Baltic coastline. This stretches for 311 miles and has broad sandy beaches. In many places along the coastline, the wind has formed dunes, or hills of sand. In other places, sea currents have carried the sand and built it up into long ridges with banks that are known as spits. In a few areas the sea has eroded the land, forming cliffs. This erosion has been a gradual process for many centuries and is still occurring today. The remains of the church walls in the village of Trzęsacz are a good example of erosion. They now stand right on the cliff edge, but two hundred years ago the church was located about 1.25 miles from the coast!

▼ The Vistula flows through the middle of the country and is the longest river in Poland (667 miles).

Sometimes, the spits cut off the gulfs from the sea and they become coastal lakes. Over the years, the saltwater fish that once lived in them have slowly adapted to the fresh water. The biggest coastal lake in Poland is Łebsko. The Łebska Spit cuts the lake off from the sea and has dunes that stretch to more than 130 feet high, the highest in the Baltic region. The wind is actually moving these dunes eastward at a rate close to two inches per year. The dunes are moving over an area that was once a forest. The sand covers the trees, depriving them of air and causing them to die slowly. You can still see the remains of old trees sticking out of the surface of the sand. In ancient times, a Slavic tribe called the Słowiński people inhabited this area. Some remnants of their way of life, including agricultural tools, have been found. The Słowiński National Park, which covers some of this region, takes its name from the tribe. The park attracts around 800,000 visitors a year. They go to see the impressive sand dunes and coastal lakes, as well as the diversity of plant and animal life that flourish there.

▲ The fishing port of Łeba lies in the eastern part of the Łebska Spit and is a popular tourist destination.

▼ Lagoons and lakes have formed behind the broad sand banks and high dunes of the coastline. This lagoon is located near the town of Elbląg in the north of Poland.

Flat plains make up the eastern part of the coast region – the delta of the Vistula River – called Żuławy Wiślane. This was shaped by the tributaries and canals around the Vistula. The landscape there is similar to the flat coastal areas of the Netherlands. This may be why it attracted Dutch settlers, who moved to Poland in the nineteenth century. They brought with them new farming techniques, including drainage systems, that improved the agricultural potential of the region.

The Lake District

In the northeast of Poland lies the Lake District, which has the most diverse landscape. Here there are moraines, post-glacial lakes, and rich forests. The soil here is very sandy,

◀ The Mazurian Lakes form the eastern part of the Polish Lake District. The lakes are joined by a series of river channels and canals. People come here to enjoy water sports such as sailing and to admire the views.

though, which is not useful for agriculture. The lakes are various shapes and sizes and lie in the small valleys created by hills. These hills reach an average height of 492 feet. The Lake District is divided by the Vistula River into two regions. The western part is called the Pomeranian Lake District and the eastern part is known as the Mazurian Lake District. Both are popular tourist areas, not only because of the beauty of the landscapes, but also because of the lively ethnic culture of the local people. The district of the Great Mazurian Lakes is particularly popular because of its clean environment. It has been nicknamed the "green lungs of Poland," and is a paradise for fans of sailing and fishing.

Uplands and mountains

As you travel southward in Poland, the landscape becomes more mountainous. The areas known as the uplands are really the foothills of the mountains that lie in the far south of the country. The landscape is varied across this region. In Upper Silesia, for example, land use is mainly industrial, while the Lublin Uplands are largely agricultural.

The Świętokrzyskie Mountains rise in south-central Poland, while farther to the south, the much taller Carpathian Mountains form a natural border with Slovakia. To the southwest, the Sudeten Mountains border the Czech Republic. From the highest mountain in the Tatra range of the Carpathians, all the different features of the landscape can be seen, including sharp ridges, high snowy peaks, rivers, and deep valleys formed by the ancient glaciers. Both the uplands and the mountain regions of Poland are popular with walkers and climbers for their peace and quiet and their breathtaking views.

▶ The Carpathian Mountains lie in the south of Poland on the border with Slovakia, where the highest peak is Gerlach (8,737 feet).

Towns and cities

Warsaw is both the capital of Poland and of the country's largest province, Mazovia. It is also the biggest city in Poland, with around 1.6 million residents. Warsaw is home to many important church and state buildings, including religious centers, government offices, and foreign embassies.

▲ *Warsaw is developing rapidly today. Modern skyscrapers are being built in the center, and shopping malls are appearing on the outskirts of the city.*

▼ *The statue in the middle of Castle Square in Warsaw is the oldest monument in the city. It was erected in 1644 and commemorates King Sigismund Vasa III.*

Warsaw

Warsaw is one of Poland's greatest cultural centers and has been the main location for some of the country's most dramatic events. Several times in the past, patriotic inhabitants of Warsaw fought against invaders. The city was severely damaged during the German occupation in World War II, when 20 percent of the population was killed and 60 percent of the buildings were destroyed. Many of the buildings have now been carefully repaired or rebuilt, and Warsaw is a fascinating and thriving city once more. Several older monuments miraculously survived the war. Among these is the Wilanów Palace, built for King Jan Sobieski III in the seventeenth century. The Royal Castle (below) was not so lucky, and was completely destroyed in the war. It was rebuilt in a very grand style in the 1970s and marks the beginning of the famous Royal Route between Castle Square and the two palaces of Wilanów and Lazienki.

Gdańsk

Gdańsk lies in the very north of Poland. It is believed to have been founded in the year 997 by Prince Mieszko I. The earliest inhabitants of the area were Eastern Europeans who traveled across the Baltic Sea in search of amber, a kind of gem. The succeeding generations of Poles, Dutch, and Germans all contributed to the unique beauty of the town. As with many other Polish cities, Gdańsk was seriously damaged during World War II. Many of the current structures are the result of rebuilding in the second half of the twentieth century. Some parts of the old town exist, however, including the Mariacki Church and several beautiful houses.

Gdańsk is mainly an industrial town. The biggest enterprises are the oil refinery and the shipyard, where the famous Solidarity movement was born (see page 46). A monument stands at the gate of the shipyard to commemorate the event.

▲ *This hoisting crane is one of the monuments of old Gdańsk that survived the war.*

▼ *Situated in the very north of Poland, on the Baltic Sea, Gdańsk is a thriving port.*

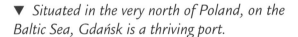

This young boy is a street musician. He and his brother play music in the market square. "I have been playing the violin since I was six," he explains when he stops for a break. "I am 14 now and still go to school. When classes are over, my brother and I go to our regular spot to play. Although most people know us, they don't give us any money. For that we depend on tourists, who can be very generous." There are many street entertainers making money from tourists in towns and cities across Poland.

Elbląg

Elbląg, in the eastern part of the Polish lowlands, is an old seaport connected with the Mazurian Lake District by the Elbląski River. The town was founded in 1237 by the Teutonic Knights, although at that time it was part of Prussia, not the Polish state. Along with many historical sites (several of which have been restored since the war), Elbląg is famous for its parks and gardens. There is also a lot to see in the surrounding area, including a Teutonic castle at Malbork. The town hosts a music festival in the summer that is very popular with locals and tourists alike.

▲ Elbląg is a popular tourist destination. This town plan shows the key sites for visitors.

▶ Trams like this one in Elbląg are a common sight in the towns and cities of Poland.

Poznań

Poznań lies in the center of Greater Poland (*Wielkopolska*). This was once the heart of the Polish state where the ruler of Poland, Mieszko I, converted to Christianity more than 1,000 years ago. The cathedral built on that site is one of the most important monuments in the city. Poznań is host to the International Trade Fair, which began in 1922 and has become one of the most prestigious events of its kind.

Gniezno

Gniezno is one of the oldest towns in Poland. Its history stretches back to the birth of the Polish state. In the year 1000, Otto III, the German emperor, met the Polish ruler Boleslaus the Brave. The meeting is known as the "Summit of Gniezno." The two rulers established the first Polish archbishopric, giving the archbishop religious power over Gniezno, and Boleslaus the Brave was awarded the right to be crowned as the first king of Poland. Gniezno thus became Poland's first capital, and Polish kings were crowned there for more than 300 years.

There are many historical sites in Gniezno, including the great cathedral, which dates from the fourteenth century. In the cathedral lies the tomb of St. Adalbertus, a bishop who was murdered while trying to convert a Prussian tribe living in the Mazurian Lake District to Christianity. In more recent times, Gniezno has become a symbol of the reconciliation between Poland and Germany after World War II. Every few years, conferences are held at Gniezno that are attended by key church officials and politicians from both countries.

Sixty-two percent of the Polish population lives in cities. There are many small towns, however, with a population of less than 5,000. A city with more than 200,000 inhabitants is considered big. Warsaw, the capital city, has more than one and a half million people.

▼ *The old market square in Poznań has been a meeting place for traders from both east and west for more than 1,000 years.*

◄ The Branicki Palace in Białystok lies in the center of the city and is the Branicki family residence. The palace has been nicknamed "The Versailles of the North."

Białystok

Located in northeastern Poland, Białystok is the capital of the province with the same name. One of the most striking features of the city is the mixture of traditions from Eastern and Western Europe and its ethnic and religious diversity. This is reflected most notably in its church buildings: there are Roman Catholic, Greek Catholic, and Orthodox churches. In the surrounding area, there are also villages populated by Islamic Tartars.

Katowice

Katowice, in southern Poland, is a typical industrial town. It began to grow and prosper in the middle of the nineteenth century due to the building of the Berlin railway that ran from Germany through Poland. It is a thriving modern town whose industrial nature is evident among the housing estates, factory chimneys, and mine-hoist towers, similar to elevators built in mine shafts. The town is also a renowned cultural and scientific center, home to the University of Silesia and the Provincial Park of Culture and Recreation.

Łódź

Though Łódź is a relatively new city, it is now the third largest in the country. Located right in the middle of Poland, Łódź was founded 200 years ago when its textile industry began to develop. Soon it became a center of international trade. The main street has many houses built in the decorative and ornamental style that was typical of the second half of the nineteenth century. Łódź is also home to Poland's film school and one of the country's finest museums of modern art. On the outskirts of the city is the medieval village of Piotrków Trybunalski.

▶ Łódź is best known for its industrial architecture, such as cotton mills, but it also has several other fine structures, like this baroque church.

Częstochowa

Częstochowa is regarded as the spiritual capital of Poland. Every year, thousands of Catholics make a pilgrimage to the monastery of Jasna Góra ("Bright Mountain"). During the "Swedish Flood," when invaders overpowered most of Poland, only Jasna Góra remained untaken. This was due to its location on a hill near the city and the determination of the monks who defended it. The famous painting *The Lady of Częstochowa* (also known as the "Black Madonna") is housed here and is worshipped by Catholic pilgrims not only from Poland, but also from neighboring countries. They come on foot to Częstochowa during the major religious festival in August.

Wrocław

Wrocław, on the Oder River in southwest Poland, is a city full of parks and historic architecture. The biggest zoo in Poland can be found here.

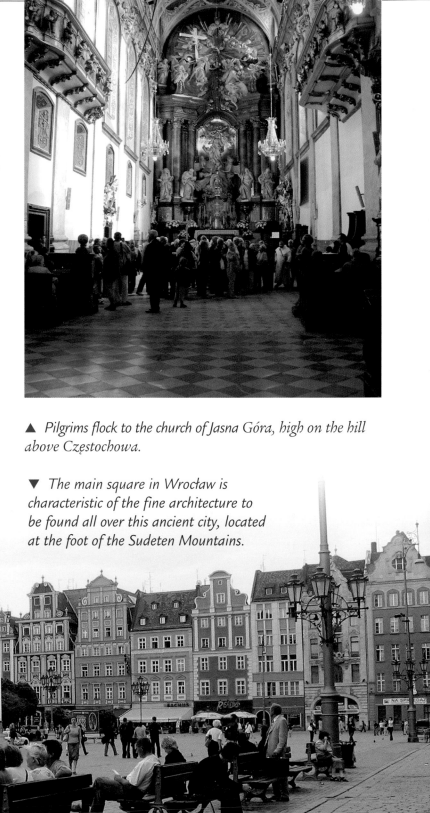

▲ Pilgrims flock to the church of Jasna Góra, high on the hill above Częstochowa.

▼ The main square in Wrocław is characteristic of the fine architecture to be found all over this ancient city, located at the foot of the Sudeten Mountains.

▲ The citizens of Kraków wanted to build a church to rival the royal cathedral on Wawel Hill, so they constructed this: the Church of Our Lady.

▲ Wawel Cathedral has no fewer than 18 chapels and is the final resting place of many Polish kings.

Kraków

Kraków is one of the most beautiful cities in Poland and has served as the country's capital for centuries. The most famous building in Kraków is the Royal Castle on Wawel Hill. The site itself is ancient. People lived there more than 3,000 years ago. The present castle was built in the sixteenth century for King Sigismund I, although Polish kings had lived in Kraków for more than 500 years before that. The center of Kraków was once surrounded by fortified walls, parts of which can still be seen today. The best preserved sections of the ancient fortress are the Barbakan stronghold and the Floriańska Gate.

Wieliczka

Wieliczka lies in southern Poland. The town is famous for its salt mine, which has been in use for more than 700 years. In the eighteenth century, a visitor to the mines commented that it was as magnificent as the Egyptian pyramids! Salt used to be a valuable trading product and Wieliczka was the heart of a thriving industry.

◀ Despite the persecution of Polish Jews during World War II, many of Kraków's synagogues survived.

The mine is a complex system of underground galleries, stretching for more than 124 miles, which connect around 2,000 "rooms" or caverns across nine different levels. Over the centuries, mineworkers developed a tradition of carving statues in the salt. The result of this centuries-old custom is an underground city made up of churches, altars, reliefs, and statues. There is an underground museum and even a health spa built in the mine. People visit the spa believing that the air in the mine, saturated with salt, has a healing effect, particularly for those suffering from illnesses like bronchitis.

The Wieliczka salt mine has become part of UNESCO's World Heritage list due to its unique nature and historic and artistic value. Every year, around one million visitors go to marvel at the sight.

▲ *The salt mine in Wieliczka is a maze of huge caverns with statues and reliefs all carved out of the salt.*

▼ *The town of Zakopane lies in the foothills of the Tatra mountain range.*

Zakopane

Zakopane's mountain scenery once attracted writers and artists, but today it is more popular for hikers and skiers. Despite being a great tourist spot, the town is famous for maintaining many regional traditions. Visitors to Zakopane can hear ethnic music and dialects and also try a number of traditional dishes.

People and culture

Poland has a population of nearly 40 million. More than 97 percent of these people are native Poles, while the remaining three percent is made up of other ethnic groups. In Europe, only Greece and Portugal have smaller minority populations.

Poland's minorities include Germans (around 153,000), Belarusians (50,000), Ukrainians (31,000), and gypsies, or Roma (13,000). However, among the Polish natives there are several different ethnic groups that each have their own traditions. These groups include the Silesians, Kashubs, and Górale

"My friend is getting married. In Poland, it is traditional for guests to take flowers to the ceremony and present them to the couple. After the service, there will be a reception where we will have a meal and dance to lively polka music."

▼ It is traditional to pin money to the bride's dress at a wedding. Here, a bride and groom collect coins that have been tossed outside the church for good luck.

(mountaineers). These groups can be distinguished not only by their varying customs, but also by slight differences in language. On special occasions, Polish people wear colorful national costumes. The most spectacular are those worn by people from the Kraków and Łowicz regions, as well as the mountaineers.

A mature society

Poland is considered to be a "mature" society. This means that it has a high percentage of older people. There are more children (up to the age of 15) than people over 65. However, the percentage of young people is decreasing every year, while the number of old people is increasing as people live longer. Poland's average life expectancy is 80 years for women and 71 years for men. The country has quite a low birthrate, meaning more people are dying than are being born. Poland also has a migration deficit. That is, more people emigrate abroad than migrate to the country.

Poles abroad

Twelve million Polish people live in other countries. The majority of them – around eight million – have emigrated to the U.S. Cities such as Chicago, Detroit, and New York have large Polish populations. Germany has more Polish immigrants than any other European country – around 1.5 million.

▲ *Folk musicians in national dress playing in the market square in Poznań*

Although the rate of unemployment in Poland is high (around 20 percent), the quality of life in the country is not poor. The number of Poles owning cars and other technologies such as computers has increased dramatically in the past few years. Fifteen million people in Poland now own mobile phones. Poles also enjoy better health than people in many other European countries.

◄ *The average age of the Polish population is increasing as people are living longer, but the birthrate is declining.*

Religion in Poland

The majority of Polish people (around 95 percent) are Roman Catholics. The Church plays an important part in the spiritual lives of many Poles. For example, more than 75 percent attend church services regularly. During the Partitions of the eighteenth century (see page 7), the Church helped the people preserve a sense of national identity and played a significant role in regaining independence. It also provided spiritual support for many Poles during the communist regime after World War II.

There are a number of other Churches in Poland, including the Greek and Russian Orthodox and Protestant denominations. The largest Protestant denomination is the Lutheran-Augsburg Church.

St. Andrew's Night

One of Poland's most popular holidays is St. Andrew's Night, or *Andrzejki*, which is celebrated on November 30. Traditionally, on this day young Polish people tell one another's fortunes. To do this, they switch off the lights and light a candle. Holding the candle over a bowl of cold water, they let some hot wax drip into the water. It hardens and forms a shape that floats on the surface. The fortune teller then "reads" or interprets the shape to reveal what the coming year will bring. The custom began many years ago when it was intended to predict the future of unmarried girls, particularly their prospects for a good marriage.

National symbols

Poland's national colors are white and red. The choice of these colors dates back to the pennants used by medieval kings. They are represented in the national flag as two equally sized horizontal bands. The top half is white and the bottom red. The national emblem depicts a white eagle (the symbol of the Piast dynasty) with a gold crown on the red background. The national anthem, Dabrowski's *Mazurek*, expresses love for the country and faith in the strength of its people.

Government

Poland is a democratic state. The parliament consists of two chambers (called *Sejm* and *Senat*) and members are elected every four years. They are the highest levels of legislative authority. Executive power is exercised by the government and the president. The president is the head of state and the supreme commander of the armed forces. General elections are held in Poland every five years.

▲ A nun speaks to a young girl in the street. Religion plays a large part in most people's lives.

◀ The currency in Poland is the złoty. This is a 100 złoty bill, which is equivalent to about 33 U.S. dollars.

The country is divided into 16 provinces. Each province is run by a governor appointed by the government and a provincial assembly elected by the citizens. The provinces are made up of districts, which are subdivided into communes. Districts and communes are units of self-government.

Today, Poland maintains good relationships with all its neighboring countries and is very active in the international arena. It was one of the founding members of the United Nations and its army participates in many peace missions, including Kosovo, Afghanistan, and Iraq. As mentioned earlier, Poland is a member of NATO and, since May 1, 2004, of the European Union.

Famous Poles

One of the most well-known Poles is Nicolas Copernicus (1473–1543). He was the first person to suggest that the Earth moved around the Sun, which was contrary to what most people believed at that time. Other famous Polish scientists include Marie Curie (1867–1934), who discovered the chemical elements radium and polonium. Fryderyk Chopin (1810–49) is also a much-loved Polish pianist and composer. The most famous Pole of the twentieth century was Pope John Paul II (see page 47).

▼ *A statue of Nicolas Copernicus (left), a portrait of Fryderyk Chopin (middle), and a photograph of Marie Curie (right)*

Education

Poland has a good education system and Polish children receive the same standard of education as those in Western Europe. There are five levels of education, with the same system across the whole country.

The first stage is kindergarten for children ages three to five. After kindergarten, children move on to primary school until the age of 13. They do not take any exams at the end of this stage. Then they move on to lower secondary school until they are 16. Primary and lower secondary schools are compulsory in Poland, meaning all children must attend school between the ages of five and 16. At the end of lower secondary school, pupils take exams to go on to further education. Further education falls into two categories: general secondary schools and vocational secondary schools. These are for children ages 17 to 19.

▼ *Nicola attends this primary school in Gdańsk. She will leave when she is 13 and move on to a lower secondary school.*

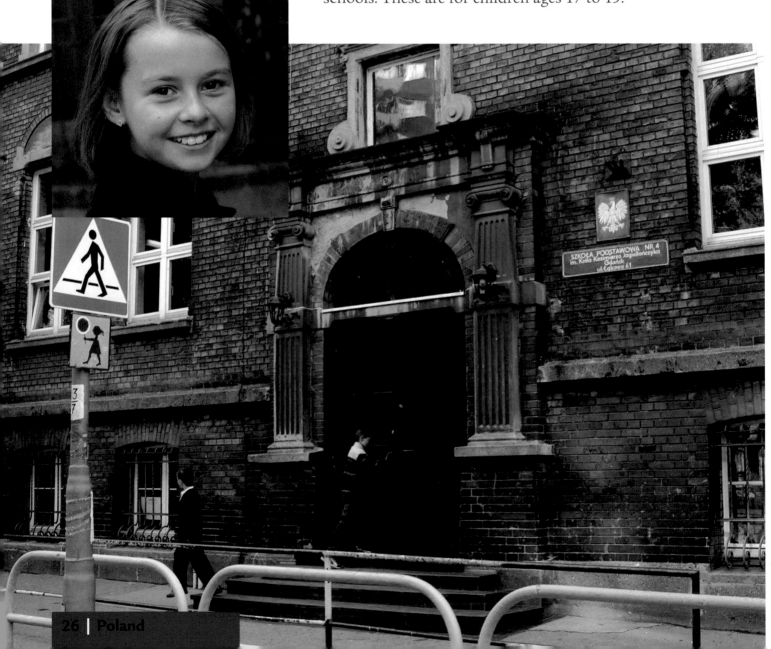

◀ *Children play outside of a village school.*

School years last almost 10 months and are divided into two semesters. The school year begins on September 1 and ends in the middle of June. The summer vacation lasts throughout July and August. Pupils have other breaks at Christmas, New Year, and Easter. There is another short break in January or February. The school week begins on Monday and ends on Friday or Saturday, depending on the local authorities.

Exams

Exam results help to determine whether a student attends a general or vocational secondary school. Vocational schools focus on practical subjects, while general secondaries are more academic. Although this stage is not compulsory, most Polish children continue their education. The exams students take at the end of upper secondary level can gain them admission to universities.

At the moment, many young people in Poland take their education as far as they can. They realize that a better education will improve their chances of getting a job.

▶ *The University of Warsaw was established in 1816.*

Although there is an education curriculum in Poland, it is quite flexible. The Ministry of Education sets up the minimum requirements at each stage and this forms the basis for the syllabus. However, the teachers can adapt the syllabus to suit the conditions of the school and the needs and abilities of the students. This is also true of the textbooks that are used in schools, although they have to be approved by the Ministry of Education. There are no fees for attending a public school, but pupils have to buy their own textbooks and take them to school every day.

▼ This lesson plan shows some typical weekly lessons for a pupil in a lower secondary school (between the ages of 13 and 16). The optional classes at the end of the day might be extra foreign language lessons or sports.

The number of lessons in a week depends on the age of the pupils. There are usually 23 lessons per week in primary schools, 28 in lower secondary schools, and 31 in general and vocational secondary schools. The curriculum includes several core subjects, such as math, the three sciences (biology, chemistry, and physics) and Polish language. Many schools also place importance on technological subjects such as IT (information technology).

Typical lesson plan for a lower secondary school

	Monday	Tuesday	Wednesday	Thursday	Friday
1	math	chemistry	English	art	Polish
2	biology	math	physics	geography	Polish
3	Polish	English/PE (in groups)	religion	English/PE (in groups)	physics
4	English/PE (in groups)	Polish	math	Polish	English/PE (in groups)
5	geography	history	math		lesson with class teacher
6	history	technology	PE		biology
7					civic education
8	optional classes				

Another important subject is foreign languages. Students are required to study at least one language throughout their education. Teaching of foreign languages begins in the fourth year of primary school. The most common languages learned in Polish schools are English, German, Russian, and French. Some schools also offer lessons in Spanish or Italian. Religious Studies (Roman Catholicism) is taught as an optional subject in schools. Students also have three lessons of physical education per week.

It is possible to specialize in particular areas by taking classes that are grouped as "paths." These are made up of similar subjects. Humanities includes Polish, foreign languages, history, and social studies. The Mathematical and Natural Science path consists of math, biology, geography, physics, and chemistry. There are also paths that cover issues such as environmental education, art, European education, and intercultural education. These are very popular among students in Polish schools, as is computer studies.

The school day

School starts at eight o'clock and each lesson lasts 45 minutes. The number of students in each class depends on the location of the school. In busy towns and cities there can be up to 40 pupils per class, but there may be only half that number in schools in rural areas. Across the whole country there is an average of 21 students in each class.

After the normal lessons of the day, pupils can take part in optional classes, such as sports. Learning foreign languages (particularly English) in additional classes is becoming increasingly common. Learning how to use the Internet is also popular. Internet use is not only educational, but also provides entertainment and helps to develop students' personal interests.

◀ *A small primary school in Rybnik in southern Poland*

▲ *These pupils are studying at a famous forestry school in Bialowieza, a vocational secondary school.*

Many Polish children live in small villages in the countryside where there are no schools, so they often have to commute to the nearest town. They take special buses, which are free of charge, called *gimbuses*. The name comes from the words *gimnazjum* (the Polish name for lower secondary school) and autobus. They are painted bright orange so they can be seen from a distance. The journey to school can be time consuming, however. Children in villages often help their parents on their farms, so their school day can be long and tiring.

School uniforms are not obligatory in Poland and only a few schools have them. Usually, pupils are allowed to wear their own clothes.

"We go to school in Braniewo," Amanda tells us.

"There are no schools in our village, so every day we take the school bus to town and back," her friend Elizabeth adds.

"We get up early every morning because the bus arrives at 7 o'clock," Amanda explains.

"We have had a lovely two-month vacation, but school starts again next week," Elizabeth says. However, the girls don't mind going back to school. They can get bored during the long summer months.

Cuisine

One of the best ways to understand a country and its culture is to learn about its food and the favorite dishes the people cook. In Poland, some of the most delicious meals are the traditional dishes from different regions.

Polish cuisine is quite heavily influenced by other cultures. In Poland today you can taste dishes from all over the world. Foreign delicacies were first introduced in the houses of the nobility from people who traveled and then brought back new ideas to Poland. Gradually, the influences of Italian, French, Russian, Hungarian, and Jewish cooking began to show up in the Polish kitchen.

What we would call modern Polish cuisine became popular in the nineteenth century. Traditional dishes are now passed down from generation to generation. Eating habits and recipes are strongly connected with the climate, culture, and religion of a region.

▼ *This cheese stand is advertising a Polish speciality,* oscypek, *cheese made from sheep's milk.*

Kraków sausage is probably the best-known sausage in Poland. According to the Polish recipe, it is made of 80 percent pork, 10 percent beef and 10 percent fat. It is seasoned with pepper, fresh garlic, and cumin. The sausage is smoked in hot smoke until it is golden brown and then braised or cooked. After it has been left to cool down, it is smoked again in warm smoke that gives it a dark brown color.

Traditional Polish foods include a variety of soups (hot and cold), sauerkraut (pickled cabbage), pickled cucumber, potatoes, pork, and dairy products, such as cheese.

Popular dishes are *bigos* (sliced sausage, pork and beef stewed in sauerkraut), *pierogi* (dumplings), goat's cheese, mushrooms, tripe, sirloin, and different sausages.

▲ Żurek is a sour soup made with egg and sausage.

Poland has applied for European Union certificates that will allow the country to produce regional products according to original recipes and sell them across Europe. Such products include *oscypek*, plum vodka from Nowy Sącz, some kinds of dried or smoked sausages, mushroom dishes, fruit and vegetable preserves, soups such as barszcz, dishes made of potatoes, and various kinds of *pierogi*.

Christmas

Christmas and Easter are very important in Poland. They are not only celebrated as religious festivals when families get together. They are also the times when many customs are observed, including the cooking of traditional dishes.

Christmas Eve is the most important evening of the year. It starts when the first star appears in the sky. All members of the family sit at the table and share special wafers. This custom, unique to Poland, is based on the ancient tradition of families sharing bread and is an important Polish tradition. The table is set with a tablecloth and candles so the meal looks festive. Many people still put a handful of hay under the tablecloth to remind them of the stable in Bethlehem. An extra place is always set for an unexpected guest.

Recipe for barszcz

Ingredients
12 medium-sized beets
1 onion, chopped
1/4 cup of water
The juice of 1 lemon
1 teaspoon of sugar
1 cup of vegetable broth
Salt and pepper
1/2 cup of sour cream

Wash the beets. Peel them and cook them with the onion in the water until they are soft. Add the lemon juice, sugar, salt, and pepper. Let the mixture stand overnight. Blend it and add the broth. Heat the mixture and add the sour cream before serving.

Traditional dishes eaten on Chrismas Eve include mushroom soup with noodles, fish soup with cream and noodles, or beet soup with small dumplings stuffed with mushrooms. Fish is also popular and different types are eaten at this time of year, such as carp or herring, either cooked in jelly, fried, or served with a sauce. The traditional cabbage and dumplings or noodles are also served with mushrooms or poppy seeds. For dessert, the Poles eat dried fruit in syrup, such as cranberries, or poppy seeds with honey or poppy-seed pie, gingerbread, or cookies.

▲ *Christmas is an important holiday in Poland and festive decorations are put on the table.*

Easter

Easter, the most important holiday in the Christian tradition, begins with the blessing of the food. A great deal of effort goes into preparing Easter breakfast, which consists of several cold dishes. On Holy Saturday, the day before Easter, the Poles carry baskets to church so they can be blessed. The baskets contain samples of everything they will have for breakfast: a leg of lamb decorated with a red flag, twigs and flowers, eggs, sausage, slices of ham, pastry, salt, pepper, and horseradish. All these items have a symbolic meaning. The lamb with the flag symbolizes Christ, while the twigs, flowers, and eggs stand for the new life that Christ gives through His Resurrection. The tradition of blessing the Easter breakfast began in the twelfth century. Until the eighteenth century, priests would actually visit people's homes to bless the meal. Since then, though, it has become more practical to take a basket to church.

One of the most traditional Easter foods is hardboiled eggs. These are often painted or patterns are scratched on the shell. Patterns vary depending on the region. The customary meat to eat at Easter is pork in varying forms. Smoked or boiled ham is popular. Boiled or roasted white sausages, often served with grated horseradish and vinegar or lemon juice, are also particularly popular. The Poles have a traditional Easter cake called *mazurek*, made of cream, nuts, raisins, and dried fruit on a wafer base.

Eating out

Eating out has become popular in Poland in the past few years. Under the communist regime, eating at restaurants was not encouraged. Today, however, Poland has a fast-food culture like many other nations. American and Asian dishes are served in numerous fast-food restaurants. Traditional European cuisine, especially Italian and French, is also becoming popular. A recent trend, which has benefited locals and the tourist trade, has been the opening of new restaurants that specialize in typical Polish food. A traditional saying in Poland is "a hungry Pole is an angry Pole."

◄ *A breaded pork chop with sauerkraut and potatoes*

Transportation

Poland lies right in the heart of Europe. This means that the shortest routes from Eastern to Western Europe, and from north to south, cut right through Poland. The fact that much of the country is made up of flat lowlands has helped with the building of roads and railways.

▼ Signs indicating main roads are green with white writing. The route numbers are white in a dark rectangle.

Two of the most important road routes are the A2, which runs from Germany to the Russian capital Moscow, and the A4, which runs from Germany to Lvov and Kiev in Ukraine. Two new roads are being built with the help of funding from the European Union. These will run from Estonia, Latvia, and Lithuania to Warsaw, and from Gdańsk to the southern border and as far as the Adriatic Sea.

▼ People use buses or trams to travel around locally.

◀ A small train, typical of those that run on local lines

Most people in Poland travel by car. The number of people owning cars has increased dramatically in recent years. By 2002, there were 300 cars per 1,000 inhabitants, which is close to Europe's average. There are more than 226,800 miles of roads across Poland, but only about 250 miles of these are freeways.

Railways

Poland has more railway tracks than most European countries, but in recent years the transportation of people and goods by rail has declined, as more people travel by road. It is really only the busy main railway lines that are profitable. The smaller lines are slowly closing down. At the same time, railway tracks that can accommodate new high-speed trains are being built or modernized. These will run from Warsaw to other key Polish cities, including Kraków, Katowice, Wrocław, Poznań, Szczecin, and Gdańsk. These intercity trains can reach speeds of 100 mph and are cheaper and quicker than traveling by car. In many cases, they are even better than traveling by plane. Equally fast Euro City trains link Warsaw to Berlin, Moscow, Prague, and Bratislava.

▲ An intercity train stops at Swarzedz station. These high-speed trains are being introduced across Poland.

Shipping

Polish shipping has undergone significant changes, including the former state merchant marine fleet being taken into private ownership. Economic zones were established, meaning that the Polish deep-sea fishing fleet could no longer

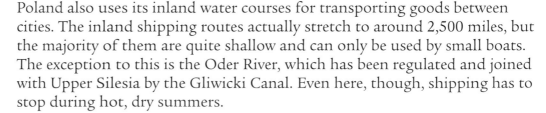

▲ *From Gdańsk it is possible to take a ferry to Nynäshamn, just south of Stockholm in Sweden.*

fish anywhere it liked. It has since had to be closed down. Today, only a few fishing boats patrol the small "Polish" fishing zone in the Baltic.

Transportation by sea is well established in Poland. There are three main ports on the Baltic coast in the north: Gdańsk, Gdynia, and Szczecin-Świnoujście. Ferries owned by Polish companies, as well as those from other European countries, sail regularly from Świnoujście and Gdynia to Sweden and Denmark. However, the ports used to serve many more ships than they do now. The decrease in traffic in Poland's ports is largely due to the drop in the importance of coal in foreign trade. Coal used to be Poland's most important and profitable export and was mass produced and shipped to countries all over Europe, but today there is far less demand for coal.

Poland also uses its inland water courses for transporting goods between cities. The inland shipping routes actually stretch to around 2,500 miles, but the majority of them are quite shallow and can only be used by small boats. The exception to this is the Oder River, which has been regulated and joined with Upper Silesia by the Gliwicki Canal. Even here, though, shipping has to stop during hot, dry summers.

▼ *LOT is Poland's national airline company.*

Aviation

LOT is Poland's national airline. It has a fleet of 50 long-distance aircraft, connecting Poland with 27 other countries. There are three international airports in Poland located in Warsaw, Kraków, and Gdańsk. The Fryderyk Chopin airport in Warsaw is particularly convenient, as it is located only four miles from the city center. The most popular destinations from Poland are the United States and Canada. Domestic flights are less popular, since for many inland journeys, traveling by train is just as fast and much cheaper.

The economy

The structure of the economy in Poland is similar to other European countries. It is divided between services (66 percent), industry (31 percent), and agriculture (3 percent). The economy has stabilized over the past decade and since joining the European Union, Poland has received funding that should improve the economy further.

▼ *A farmer uses his bicycle to herd cattle down a street in Bialowieza.*

Agriculture

Poland produces enough food to supply its population and allow a surplus. The country's climate, landscape, and soil create good conditions for growing crops and breeding cattle and other livestock. There is a lot of farmland in Poland, equal to nearly 1.25 square miles per person. Farming in Poland, however, is not done as efficiently as in many other European countries. There are too many small farms and too many people employed on them. An average farm in Poland is about 20 acres and 11 percent of the population are farmers.

Many of the smaller farms find it hard to make enough money, so some farmers take on additional employment. Some even turn their farms into tourist attractions. Here, people who live in cities

can go and see how people in the country live and taste regional dishes. Children can learn that milk comes from cows, not containers!

The majority of small farms use traditional methods of growing crops and breeding farm animals. As a result, agricultural products are healthy and free from artificial products. Many farmers use only natural or ecologically safe fertilizers and pesticides.

◀ *Cabbages are harvested and then transported to market.*

Besides raising cattle, Polish farmers grow wheat, rye, potatoes, and sugar beets. Wheat requires very fertile soil, but rye and potatoes can be grown even in the northern and eastern areas, where the soil is not nearly as rich. Farmers in Poland also grow barley and oats in small quantities, as well as hops, flax, and hemp.

Another one of Poland's main crops is fruit. Apple juice from Polish apples is exported to countries all over the world. Plums, strawberries, raspberries, and black currants are also widely grown.

Raising sheep used to be common in Poland, but in recent years sheep farming has become less popular. Some farmers still keep small herds of sheep, but these are mainly in the mountains. There the sheepskins are used to make coats and the milk is used to produce the regional cheese *oscypek*.

The breeding of race horses is a long-standing tradition in Poland. Auctions of Arabian horses are held in Janów Podlaski and attract horse lovers and buyers from many different countries. Farmers all over Poland used to have horses plow the fields. Today, though, draft horses, as they are known, are decreasing. They are found mainly on farms in the mountainous regions in the south of the country.

▼ *Potatoes are one of the most important crops grown in Poland and a major export.*

▲ *In the past, Polish farmers used horses to help in the fields, but in most areas today modern machinery is used.*

▶ *A copper smelting plant in Legnica in eastern Poland*

Industry

Polish industry started to develop during the Partitions in the eighteenth century. It has declined and been rebuilt several times since then. After World War II, factories were nationalized, or placed under government control. Heavy industry, which produced equipment for other industries, developed rapidly. Light industry, which makes products for consumers, began to decline. Before long, however, it became obvious that neither type of nationalized industry was modern enough to compete with the goods

▼ *The Elbląg branch of the Alstom company builds ships and trains in this massive factory.*

produced by more developed countries. It was only in the 1990s that the process of modernization began. Many enterprises were privatized (taken from public control to private ownership) and new technologies were introduced. The process of modernization is still going on in Poland and it encompasses all areas of the country's economy.

Poland is a big producer of cars. In addition to building cars, Polish manufacturers also build spare parts for foreign car companies, such as Volkswagen, General Motors, Fiat, and Daewoo.

The industry that manufactures construction materials, especially cement, bricks, glass, and various types of plastics, is developing rapidly in Poland. Polish furniture, clothes, medicines, cosmetics, and food products are also highly valued in the world markets. Polish companies are beginning to move into the electronics and engineering industries, as well as further developing the existing industries of construction and agriculture. The future for Poland's economy is looking bright.

Energy

The production of energy and fuel in Poland is well developed. Poland is an important producer of two different types of coal: black and brown. Both of these are used to create electricity. Only two percent of electricity is produced by hydroelectric power plants.

▲ *This factory makes parts for cars, but often the cars themselves are built in other European countries or the U.S.*

None of the power plants in Poland uses oil or natural gas because there are not many domestic sources of either. The country imports oil and gas, mainly from Russia. In additon to coal, Poland also has rich deposits of sulfur and copper ores that contain useful compounds. The sulfur is turned into sulfuric acid, which is used in several different industries. Copper is a valuable metal and once the copper ore has been mined, the copper and many of its by-products can be very useful.

Import and export

Although the Polish economy is improving, Poland is partly still a developing country. Privatization and modernization of industry are steps forward, but it may be many years before the positive effects are felt. Changing industry in this way requires importing many goods from other countries. The cost of imported products is often higher than their export value. For example, the cost of importing machinery and motor vehicles is much higher than the price those products would cost if made at home. Crude oil and natural gas imported from Russia are the most expensive imports, whereas the price of coal, a Polish export, is low and getting lower.

Poland's most important trading partner is Germany. One third of Polish exports and one quarter of imports come from business with Germany. This is the only country with which Poland has a trade surplus. With other trading partners – Italy, the Netherlands, France, the United Kingdom, and Russia – Poland has a trade deficit. In addition to foreign trade, Poland's development has been helped by credit from the World Bank.

▶ *Poland has one of the largest ship-building industries in the world. This is a shipyard in Gdańsk.*

Nature

Poland is well known for its stunning and diverse landscape. Much of the country is covered by forests and home to a variety of plant and animal life. Beaches, lakes, and rivers add to the attractive scenery. The Polish government has also set aside land to create national parks that protect plant and animal life.

More than a quarter of Poland is woodland. This woodland is home to mostly coniferous forests full of pine and fir trees. Mixed forests with oak and beech trees can also be found in some parts of the country.

In the past, even more of Poland was covered by forests, but today many of these have been cut down, with the land used for farming. There have been recent moves, however, to return the land to its natural state. Areas that have little agricultural value are being reforested. These forests, fields, and meadows give shelter to many wild animals and are important to their survival.

▲ *Areas in the northeast of the country are so clean that they have been nicknamed "the green lungs of Poland."*

◄ *Air pollution spews out of the chimneys of a coal-powered plant at the Gdańsk shipyard.*

Many of the species living in these woods, fields, and meadows are endangered. The species are partially or completely under the protection of the Polish government. Grey hares were common in Poland until quite recently, but now they are in danger of extinction. They are protected by law during their breeding season. There is currently a campaign to ban the hunting of these animals.

On the other hand, the strictly protected wisents have increased in number, so some of them are being reduced. Beavers and moose are in a similar situation. The wolf population is also considered too large. In the eastern part of the country, wolves have killed large numbers of deer, and recent attacks on herds of livestock have been reported.

▼ *Autumn colors in the Bieszczady National Park*

Wisents

A wisent is a type of wild bison and Europe's largest land mammal. The story of wisents in Poland is extraordinary. In 1914, the number of wisents began to decline because they were killed for food during World War I. By 1919, after the war, the last wisent living in the wild died in the Białowieska Forest. The only remaining examples of the species lived in zoos. From these, 12 wisents suitable for breeding were selected and kept in an isolated breeding station. A few years later, in 1959, they were reintroduced to the Białowieska Forest. Five years later, the first calf was born. Soon there were so many of them in the forest that they needed to be moved to other places and some were even shot. The Białowieska Forest is still their main habitat, but wisents also live in the Bieszczady Mountains, in the Borecka Forest (the Mazurian Lake District), and in the Pilskie Woods (the Pomeranian Lake District).

National Parks

On the plains and hills of the Polish lowlands, where agriculture first developed, the remaining forests are now protected as national parks. This large area is divided into the Wielkopolska Lowlands, the Mazowiecko-Podlaska Lowlands, and the Śląska Lowlands. Here, the most pristine landscapes Poland has to offer are found: wide river valleys with natural meadows where waterfowl build their nests. Birds are protected in the Biebrza, Narew, and Ujście Wart National Parks, as well as in many other nature reserves.

▶ *Hay stacks in the Tatra Mountains during the summer*

In the Carpathian Mountains there are two national parks. In the Tatra National Park, various types of vegetation can be found depending on the elevation above sea level. Up to 4,000 feet, there are beech-fir woods, above them, pine trees, then dwarf mountain pines and meadows. Animal life includes chamois (a goat-like animal), groundhogs, bears, and eagles. In the Polish part of the Carpathians people enjoy the Pieniny Mountains. Rafting trips are organized there every summer on the Dunajec River, which is famous for its beautiful ravines. The Bieszczady Mountains are home to the Bieszczady National Park, where vast meadows and beech forests are the habitat of bears, wolves, lynx, wildcats, and wisents.

Forest-dominated national parks include the Kampinos and Białowieska. In Kampinos, bordering the capital city of Warsaw, there are moose and lynx. Both of these are being reintroduced into their natural habitat. The Białowieska National Park is also on UNESCO's World Heritage list. This is the last natural forest with wisents (see page 42).

▶ *The Suwalki Nature Reserve in eastern Poland*

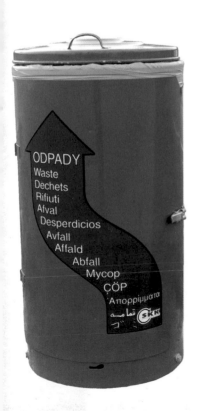

Environmental issues

Intensive development of industry occurred after 1945 and the environment suffered as a result. Industry used to be the main cause of air pollution. Almost all energy in Poland is produced from coal. In the process of burning coal, enormous amounts of pollution are created. However, over the last 10 years, power plants have installed modern filters. These filters reduce the emission of sulfur dioxide, nitrous oxide, and dust. Today, the main cause of pollution is the car. In many urban areas, the pollution from exhaust fumes makes up 60 percent of the total pollution. Water in Poland is transported by pipes for great distances and is purified using chlorine and ozone. This actually makes the water taste worse. To improve water quality, many new sewage plants have been built. Also, lakes and rivers are no longer polluted by pesticides and fertilizers because farmers are using these chemicals more carefully. In schools, Polish children participate in activities to improve the environment, such as collecting litter in forests on Earth Day and learning to separate waste into items that can be recycled and those that can't.

Tourism

Poland might not be as popular as the Mediterranean as a vacation destination, but it has a lot to offer foreign visitors. More and more people travel to Poland every year to enjoy its customs, scenery, and architecture.

▼ *Climbing is a popular sport in the mountains of southern Poland.*

Poland's rich landscape is its greatest tourist attraction. Because of this, visitors enjoy many outdoor sports, such as camping, hiking, mountain climbing, sailing, canoeing, windsurfing, bicycling, and especially skiing.

Poland's national parks are ideal for hiking. Many have marked trails and maps that are easy to follow. Hiking through the Tatra Mountains is more demanding since some climbing is involved. For water sports, or even simply swimming, the Mazurian Lake District is becoming increasingly popular. Several campground sites have been set up next to the rivers and lakes. In northern Poland, bicyclists enjoy the landscape because there aren't many hills and the roads are not very busy.

Poland's main skiing destinations are to the south of Katowice in Zakopane and Szczyrk. Although there can be long waits at these destinations, they are often less expensive than skiing in the Alps.

Those looking for souvenirs to remember their time in Poland will have no trouble. Shopping centers similar to American shopping malls are increasing in many cities, but street merchants are also quite active. Souvenirs of painted wooden eggs, pottery, embroidered tablecloths, and hand-carved figurines are popular. Unlike some other cultures, Polish people tend not to haggle over prices. Typically, the price that is displayed is the price merchants expect to be paid.

Cultural attractions

The outdoors is not all that Poland has to offer. There are more than 600 museums in Poland. Tours of historical sites, such as Auschwitz and Stutthof, two infamous concentration camps of World War II, draw many visitors. Poland is also the homeland of the famous nineteenth-century classical composer Fryderyk Chopin (see page 25). Chopin was born in Zelazowa Wola, near Warsaw, and his childhood home, an inn, has now been turned into a museum dedicated to him. Internationally known current composers often give concerts in a park near Chopin's birthplace.

Another famous historical site is the enamelware operation called Emalia in Kraków that was run by Oskar Schindler. At risk to himself, Schindler, a German businessman, employed hundreds of Jews to work in his factory during World World II. Forced labor in Schindler's factory spared Jews from death and the horrors of Nazi concentration camps.

The violet

A Polish legend tells the story of the violet. Set in the kingdom of Wends, the story tells of a Slavic tribe that lived on the borders of the River Elbe. Long ago, an evil god, Czorneboh, ruled the Wends. He brought them nothing but suffering. Czorneboh, however, had a lovely daughter. When the Christian missionaries came to the kingdom, Czorneboh did all he could to resist them. But the Christians were stronger. They destroyed Czorneboh's evil power and he was transformed into a rock. His beautiful daughter responded by turning herself into a violet that blossoms once every 100 years at the foot of her father, the rock. Legend says that whoever succeeds in picking this violet on Walpurgis Night (the night from April 30 to May 1) will receive the lovely daughter as his wife with all the riches as her dowry.

Poland hosts many festivals where both tourists and locals come to enjoy many Polish customs. Some of the more popular festivals occur between the months of April and October. Most are either for music, including the Springtime Music Festival in Poznań during April, or theater, such as the International Film Festival in Kraków during June.

Another popular cultural experience includes a performance of *Halka*, a sad love story involving a poor girl from the mountains. First performed in 1857, this play, along with others, inspired patriotic feelings among Poles. It used styles found in traditional Polish music, such as the mazurka (which is also used in the national anthem) and the polonaise.

Tourist areas

The Baltic coast in Poland is famous for its vast beaches. It is a perfect place for swimming, walking, and collecting amber, which used to be called the "gold of the Baltic." Amber is rinsed out from the sand by special machines and sold in jewelry shops. The most precious pieces of amber are those with insects preserved inside them, usually flies or mosquitoes.

Poland's scenery is not limited to its natural surroundings, however. People also visit the country to admire its architecture. Although parts of many cities were destroyed during World War II and have been rebuilt since then, thousands of old buildings survive. The architecture is mainly Gothic and Baroque. Tourists also visit the churches and castles and admire the wooden shrines that are scattered all over the countryside. There are several "tourist trails," including those that take in the Cistercian monasteries as well as churches and Teutonic castles. In the east and south of Poland there are many interesting examples of wooden architecture, especially small Catholic and Eastern Orthodox churches.

Many people take part in Polish religious and cultural events and festivals. These include pilgrimages to places of religious interest, Corpus Christi Day processions, food blessings during Easter, and nativity plays at Christmas.

▼ *Kraków's well-preserved old buildings attract thousands of tourists every year.*

Democratic Poland

After World War II, Europe was divided for more than 50 years. The independent trade-union movement known as Solidarity, led by Lech Wałęsa (see below), contributed greatly to the collapse of the post-war communist regime in Poland. Since 1989, Poland has been a democratic country.

Poland held elections in June of 1989 that resulted in Tadeusz Mazowiecki becoming the country's first non-communist leader since World War II. The country was on the verge of an economic collapse and the people, who had long lived under communist rule, were still suspicous of government. Several reforms were made, including a new constitution, elimination of censorship, and the reconstruction of education systems. These reforms did not happen quickly but the Poles, true to their history, persevered.

In June 2003, the majority of Poland's citizens voted in favor of joining the European Union. On May 1, 2004, Poland and nine other countries were formally accepted as member states.

Being a member of the European Union means that Poland can strengthen its ties to Western European countries, especially Germany and France, and that Poles may seek jobs in countries far from home.

▼ *Lech Wałęsa was awarded the Nobel Peace Prize for his work with the trade union Solidarity.*

Lech Wałęsa

Lech Wałęsa was born in 1943 to a working-class family in Popovo. He trained as an electrician and went to work in the Lenin Shipyards in Gdańsk. In 1970, he made headlines when he became the new leader of the existing trade union. In 1976, however, he was fired because of his involvement in strikes at the shipyard. Wałęsa then co-founded a new trade union, Solidarność ("Solidarity"), but it was not recognized by the ruling Communist Party. In 1980, inflation made the price of meat in Poland soar, resulting in massive protests by the people. Strikes broke out everywhere and Wałęsa became the spokesman for Solidarity. To end the strike, the communist government was forced to acknowledge the trade union. This caused a great deal of publicity and Wałęsa was permitted to return to his job at the shipyard. However, the economy continued to worsen and trade unions were banned. Wałęsa was arrested and briefly imprisoned. In 1983, he was awarded the Nobel Peace Prize. In 1990, Wałęsa was elected president of Poland and resigned as leader of the Solidarity movement. The years of turmoil that followed led to his defeat in the 1995 elections.

Pope John Paul II

Not even Hollywood could have made up the story of the poor Polish boy who survived two dictatorships to become one of the most influential popes in the history of the Catholic Church. Karol Jozef Wojtyla was born in the small provincial town of Wadowice on May 18, 1920, several months after Poland had regained its independence. His mother died when he was very young and he was raised by his father, a deeply religious retired army officer. Karol was very bright and was soon the top student in his school. He was also an enthusiastic athlete and showed promise as an amateur actor. However, his life was to take a very different direction. When World War II broke out, he was forced to put aside his academic and acting careers. When the war ended, he devoted himself to his religion, becoming a priest in 1946. On Sunday, October 22, 1978, he was solemnly ordained as Pope John Paul II in St. Peter's Square in Rome. As leader of the Church, he served the Catholic people until his death in April 2005.

Tragedy

Since becoming a democratic state, Poland has had its share of political upheavals. None, however, was as tragic as that following an airplane crash on April 10, 2010. In all, 96 people, including President Lech Kaczyński, his wife, and many other military and civilian leaders were killed when a Polish Air Force plane crashed en route from Warsaw to Smolensk, Russia.

Throughout Poland's history, the Polish people have endured harsh times. Yet, the Poles have never lost their national identity and pride. They remain a nation rich in tradition and customs with a promising future.

◀ *People in Poland demonstrate their support for the country becoming a member of the European Union.*

Glossary

Archbishopric The area over which an archbishop has religious control.

Communist Someone who believes that all property and industry in a country should belong to the state.

Constitution A series of laws outlining the basic principles of a government or country.

Delta A flat area at the mouth of a river where the main river splits into smaller tributaries.

Democracy Government by officials elected by the people of a country.

Erosion The wearing away of rocks over many years by wind or water.

NATO North Atlantic Treaty Organization; an alliance signed by a group of nations in 1949, working towards international peace and security.

Nobel Prize A series of prizes awarded every year for outstanding work in specific fields, such as Science, Medicine, Literature, or Peace.

Spits Sand banks built up by sea currents.

Tributary A branch of a river that flows into the main stream.

UNESCO United Nations Educational, Scientific, and Cultural Organization, established to promote education and communication.

Index

Websites

https://www.cia.gov/library/publications/the-world-factbook/geos/pl.html
www.poland.pl
www.lonelyplanet.com/poland
www.poland.travel/en-us
http://www.worldstatesmen.org/Poland.htm

Eur

Iceland

N

W E

S

NORTH SEA

Republic
of
Ireland

United Kingdom

The Ne

Belgium

Luxem

France

Switzer

Monaco

Portugal

Spain

ATLANTIC OCEAN

MEDITERRANEA

0   500 km

0   500 miles